The Busy Boys
Matthew 21: Be Willing

CATHERINE MACKENZIE
Illustrated by Chiara Bertelli

Learn it: God is the only Saviour
CF4•K Do it: Say 'yes' to God and obey him
Find it: How long does God's love last? Psalm 136:1

Have you ever said 'Yes, I'll do that!' then forgotten all about it? Perhaps you were asked to tidy your room and got so angry you shouted, 'No I will not!' You stomped off to your room but thought later, 'I shouldn't have said that.'

So afterwards you went back and quietly did the job you were asked to do. However, maybe you're one of those people who do what they're asked to do when they're asked to do it! Well, good for you.

Jesus once spoke to a bunch of people who thought they were better than everyone else. They thought that they pleased God but really they didn't. They thought they weren't sinners — that it was other people who did bad things. Not them.

Jesus wanted these people to understand the truth, so he told a story about two boys — two brothers really. Their dad had a vineyard that needed some work, so he asked his sons for some help.

He asked the first boy, 'Son, please go and work today in the vineyard.' The boy answered and said, 'I will sir.' But he did not go.

The father also asked his second son, 'Son, please go and work today in the vineyard.' The boy answered, 'No. I will not.' But afterwards the second boy felt sorry for what he had said. So he changed his mind and went to the vineyard to work hard.

Jesus asked his listeners, 'Which of these two boys actually obeyed his father?'

They replied, 'Why it was the second boy of course.'

Jesus taught his listeners that they were like the first son. They said all the right words, but their actions were wrong. They thought they weren't sinners – but they really were.

Just because you know loads of Bible stories, go to church, are polite and nice and win all the prizes – that doesn't mean you are good. You might think you're one of the best people around. But what are you really like inside?

Perhaps you think you're better than others who don't go to church on Sunday. Reading the Bible and going to church are good things to do — but just because you do them doesn't mean you are part of God's family.

Do you really know who God is and what he is like? Do you trust him? Have you asked him to forgive you? That's what you really need to do!

You can know lots of things about someone but that doesn't always mean that you really know them. You might know someone's name, where they live, even their favourite colour, but you might not have ever spent any time with them.

So do you really know God? Is God your very best friend? Maybe you know what God wants you to do — but do you actually obey God yourself?

Everyone is a sinner and everyone needs God's forgiveness. God is the only one who can save you. Your good actions don't save you. When you die you only get to heaven because Jesus Christ took the punishment you deserve.

WHAT IS A SINNER? You are a sinner when you disobey God. God must punish sin, but he wants to save sinners from being punished. Sin will destroy you, but God wants to stop this. If you turn away from your sin and trust in God, you will be with him in heaven when you die.

In the story the younger son did the right thing, although he started off doing the wrong thing. The older son did the wrong thing, even though he made great promises in the beginning.

Some people start off knowing about God. They read the Bible and behave quite nicely. But they still put themselves first.

They want to do what they want to do. They don't want to do what God wants them to do.

But God has the power to change people so that they feel sorry for their sin. They turn away from sin and God becomes their most important love. He is so happy to have them in his family.

Which one of the sons are you? Have you been saying 'no' to God? Stop. Say 'yes' and obey him.

Have you said 'yes' to God but you still disobey him? Stop. It's no good pretending to love and obey God. You must really do it.

The two boys had one father. We have one God. We have one Saviour. He is willing to save anyone who asks him to forgive them for their sins. God can change anyone so that they trust and love him.

Christian Focus Publications

Christian Focus Publications publishes books for adults and children under its four main imprints: Christian Focus, CF4K, Mentor and Christian Heritage. Our books reflect our conviction that God's Word is reliable and Jesus is the way to know him, and live for ever with him. Our children's list includes a Sunday School curriculum that covers pre-school to early teens, and puzzle and activity books. We also publish personal and family devotional titles, biographies and inspirational stories that children will love. If you are looking for quality Bible teaching for children then we have an excellent range of Bible stories and age-specific theological books. From pre-school board books to teenage apologetics, we have it covered!

AUTHOR'S DEDICATON: To my friends and family at Kingsview Christian Centre, A.P.C.

10 9 8 7 6 5 4 3 2 1

Copyright © 2017 Catherine Mackenzie

ISBN: 978-1-5271-0094-7

Published in 2017 by Christian Focus Publications Ltd.
Geanies House, Fearn, Tain, Ross-shire, IV20 1TW, Great Britain

Illustrations by Chiara Bertelli

Cover Design: Sarah Korvemaker

Printed in Malta

All rights reserved. No part of this publication may be reproduced, stored in a retrieval system, or transmitted, in any form, by any means, electronic, mechanical, photocopying, recording or otherwise without the prior permission of the publisher or a licence permitting restricted copying. In the U.K. such licences are issued by the Copyright Licensing Agency, Saffron House, 6-10 Kirby Street, London, EC1 8TS. www.cla.co.uk

Scripture quotations are from The Holy Bible, English Standard Version, copyright © 2001 by Crossway Bibles, a division of Good News Publishers. Used by permission. All rights reserved. ESV Text Edition: 2007.